Wolf Hi

It Can't Be

Roderick Hunt

Illustrated by Alex Brychta

Great Clarendon Street, Oxford OX2 6DP

Oxford University Press is a department of the University of Oxford.
It furthers the University's objective of excellence in research, scholarship, and education by publishing worldwide in

Oxford New York

Auckland Bangkok Buenos Aires Cape Town Chennai
Dar es Salaam Delhi Hong Kong Istanbul Karachi Kolkata
Kuala Lumpur Madrid Melbourne Mexico City Mumbai Nairobi
São Paulo Shanghai Singapore Taipei Tokyo Toronto

with an associated company in Berlin

First published 2002

British Library Cataloguing in Publication Data

Data available

ISBN 0 19 919525 0

1 3 5 7 9 10 8 6 4 2

Printed in Hong Kong

Chapter 1

Gizmo was in the shopping centre with his mum. They had gone to town to buy Gizmo some new shoes for school.

'I have to go to the bank first,' said Mrs Harding. 'I won't be long.'

Suddenly a police car sped into the centre. Its lights were flashing.

Three police officers jumped out and ran into the bank. Then a second police car raced up.

'I don't think we *will* be going to the bank,' said Gizmo.

'But I have to pay some money in,' said Mrs Harding. 'What's happening?'

'Something is going on. I think there's been a bank raid,' said Gizmo.

A police officer was standing outside the bank. He was stopping people from going inside.

'Why can't we go in?' asked Mrs Harding.

'There's been an armed robbery,' said the police officer.

'Was it a gang?' asked Gizmo.

'No, just one man,' replied the officer. 'But he took a lot of money.'

'Then it's a good job I didn't pay this cash in,' said Mrs Harding. 'It might have been stolen.'

Chapter 2

Kat and Arjo were playing badminton with Loz. Loz hit a bad shot and the shuttle flew into Mr Morgan's garden.

'I'll go and get it,' said Loz.

At the end of Gran's garden there was a narrow gap in the fence. Loz tried to squeeze through it.

‘Shouldn’t you ask Mr Morgan first?’ asked Kat.

‘I can’t,’ said Loz. ‘He’s away on holiday. Gran is looking after his cat.’

The gap was too narrow for Loz. ‘I must have grown since I last did this,’ she laughed.

‘I’ll try,’ said Arjo. ‘I’m smaller than you.’

There was just room for Arjo to squeeze through. He had to crawl under a bush on the other side.

He was about to step up out of the bush, when he froze!

A man was climbing through Mr Morgan's kitchen window.

Chapter 3

Arjo watched as the man climbed in. He leaned out of the window and pulled a bag inside.

Arjo could just see part of the man's face in shadow. 'It's Mr Morgan,' he thought. 'Well, I *think* it's Mr Morgan. Perhaps he's forgotten his key. That's why he's climbing into his own house.'

Arjo darted out of the bush, grabbed the shuttle and crawled back, covering up his footprints.

‘I’m sure Mr Morgan didn’t see me,’ he said to himself.

He looked back to make sure. That was odd! The man was climbing back out of the window. Why was he doing that? He had left the bag inside.

Arjo thought about it. There was something different about the way Mr Morgan looked. But he couldn't think what it was.

Chapter 4

Soon afterwards, Gran saw Mr Morgan's car pull up outside his house.

She and Loz went round with Smuts, his cat, later in the afternoon.

'I think Gran's been spoiling her,' Loz laughed.

At that moment, two police officers came to the door.

‘There was a robbery at the bank this morning,’ said one of the police officers to Mr Morgan. ‘The man who did the robbery looks just like you.’

The other officer held out a picture. ‘This was taken by the bank’s security cameras,’ she said.

Loz caught sight of it. ‘I can’t believe it!’ she thought. ‘It *is* Mr Morgan and he’s robbing the bank.’

Chapter 5

Mr Morgan looked at the picture. He went pale. 'Is this a joke?' he asked. 'I was nowhere near the bank. I was coming back from my holiday. I left the coast this morning. I was driving home.'

‘He goes to Easton-on-Sea,’ said Gran. ‘He goes every year.’

‘So it’s taken you all day to drive fifty miles?’ said the police officer.

‘I… I… I like to take my time,’ said Mr Morgan.

'We'd like to search your house,' said the first police officer.

'Go ahead,' said Mr Morgan. 'You won't find anything.'

Gran looked at him. 'Don't worry,' she said. 'It's all a mistake. I'll make a cup of tea while they search the house.'

Chapter 6

That evening Gizmo went to Kat's house. He told Kat and Arjo about the hold-up at the bank.

'Mum was just going to pay some money in,' he said. 'But then these police cars screamed up.'

Suddenly Loz ran up. She was out of breath.

'You won't believe this,' she said.

'What?' asked Kat.

'It's Mr Morgan,' said Loz. 'He's been arrested for armed robbery.'

Kat gasped. 'Mr Morgan raiding a bank! You're joking.' she said.

'It's true,' said Loz. 'I was there when the police searched his house. They found the suit he was wearing at the time. The bag he used in the robbery was under his bed. But it was empty.'

Arjo asked them what they were talking about. He watched Kat's lips as she told him about Mr Morgan.

'They must have the wrong man,' said Kat. 'He's too old to rob banks. He's got a stiff leg. He couldn't have run away.'

Arjo's eyes widened. Too old! The man he'd seen climbing into the house didn't have a stiff leg. It *couldn't* have been Mr Morgan.

Chapter 7

‘Come on!’ shouted Arjo. He started running.

‘Arjo! Stop!’ yelled Gizmo. ‘Where are you going?’

‘It’s no good yelling,’ said Kat. ‘We’d better follow him.’

Arjo raced along the street. Kat, Gizmo and Loz chased after him.

When Arjo got to Mr Morgan's house, he ran round to the back.

'Why is he going round there?' asked Loz.

Arjo told them about the man he had seen. He pointed to the window where the man had climbed in.

Arjo said the man he had seen looked *like* Mr Morgan except that he was a lot younger.

Then he looked at the soft earth. ‘Look,’ he said. ‘A footprint.’

Chapter 8

They all hurried round to tell Gran. She listened carefully as Arjo told his story.

'So the man looked *like* Mr Morgan but he was younger,' said Gran. 'It must be Trevor – Mr Morgan's nephew. He looks just like him. He's just come out of prison.'

‘I don’t get it,’ said Kat. ‘Why would his nephew break *into* the house?’

‘He’s a bad lot. He’s always been in trouble,’ said Gran. ‘He stole money a few years ago and Mr Morgan told the police. In the end Trevor went to prison.’

‘Perhaps,’ said Loz, ‘Trevor knew Mr Morgan was away. He broke in, borrowed his suit and a bag. He made himself look like Mr Morgan. Then he did the bank robbery.’

‘And he knew Mr Morgan would get blamed,’ said Gizmo.

'Surely,' said Kat, 'nobody would believe Mr Morgan could rob a bank.'

'Well, the police did,' said Gran. 'I'll phone them. They will be interested in Arjo's story.'

Chapter 9

The police pulled Trevor in for questioning. They looked at his shoes. The shoes matched the footprint. In the end Trevor confessed. He had robbed the bank and tried to put the blame on Mr Morgan.

The next day Mr Morgan called round to thank everyone.

'The police have arrested Trevor,' said Mr Morgan. 'He had bought an airline ticket.'

'Well,' said Gran. 'Trying to frame you wasn't a very clever thing for him to do.'

Arjo was the hero. It was thanks to him that Trevor had been caught.

'Just think,' said Loz. 'If we hadn't hit that shuttle over the fence, there might have been a different ending.'